Original title:
Moods in Flight

Copyright © 2024 Creative Arts Management OÜ
All rights reserved.

Author: Olivia Sterling
ISBN HARDBACK: 978-9916-90-684-2
ISBN PAPERBACK: 978-9916-90-685-9

Solid Ground

Beneath my feet, the earth holds tight,
A steadfast friend, through day and night.
In gentle hush, it breathes my name,
A place of peace, an anchor's claim.

The trees stand guard, their roots run deep,
In nature's arms, my heart can leap.
The seasons change, yet here I find,
A solid ground, a home defined.

Flights of Solace

On wings of dreams, I take to flight,
Through clouds of doubt, into the light.
Each breath a whisper, each gust a song,
In this vast expanse, I feel I belong.

The horizon calls, a canvas wide,
With every glide, I cast aside.
The weight of worry, the chains of fear,
In the boundless sky, all feels clear.

Skylarks in the Breeze

High above, the skylarks soar,
Their melodies wrap, forevermore.
In gentle winds, they dance and play,
A symphony of joy at close of day.

With every note, my spirit flies,
Chasing sunlight, beneath the skies.
In this embrace, I lose all care,
A world of wonder, free and fair.

Gliding through the Ether

In quiet realms, I drift afar,
Through silver shadows, where dreamers are.
The ether hums a soothing tune,
A lullaby beneath the moon.

Floating softly, time stands still,
With every heartbeat, I feel the thrill.
On wings of night, I soar alone,
In whispered realms, I've found my home.

Sails in the Night

Whispers glide on oceans deep,
Beneath the moon where shadows creep.
Stars twinkle in a velvet sky,
While dreams unfurl like sails up high.

The waves hum soft a lullaby,
As night descends with a gentle sigh.
Guided by the lantern's glow,
Adrift where midnight breezes blow.

Harmonics of the Air

In every note the wind will sing,
A dance of leaves, a fluttering wing.
Melodies rise from earth so free,
Carried on whispers, wild and carefree.

As dawn brings light, the chorus swells,
Echoes of nature, where silence dwells.
Voices entwined in sweet refrain,
A symphony born in sun and rain.

Distant Horizons

Far beyond the reaching land,
Where sky and sea seem hand in hand.
A world of dreams waits just in sight,
With colors bold and pure delight.

Endless wonders call the brave,
To chase the tides, to ride the wave.
The horizon whispers, soft and low,
Of journeys taken, futures to sow.

Drift of Desires

Longing floats like petals down,
In currents deep, we wear a crown.
Every wish a ripple cast,
On waters wide, both deep and vast.

Moments lost in twilight's glow,
Echoes of what we yearn to know.
Hearts adrift, a gentle sway,
In dreams we seek and hopes we lay.

Embracing the Updraft

In the light of dawn's gentle rise,
Wings spread wide under endless skies.
Floating free, the heart sings loud,
Embracing dreams like a soft, warm shroud.

Each breath a whisper, each gust a guide,
Through currents of hope, we glide and slide.
With every swirl, a new chance to soar,
Chasing the sun, always yearning for more.

Fragile Horizons

Between the lines of dusk and dawn,
Lie fragile hopes that are barely drawn.
A canvas painted in soft pastels,
Whispers of dreams where the quiet dwells.

The horizon shimmers, a thin, gold seam,
Where shadows linger and sunlight beams.
A delicate balance, a fleeting view,
Holding our breaths for a moment or two.

Skimming Across Emotions

Like a stone skipping on a glassy lake,
Fleeting moments we choose to take.
Each touch connects, a spark of the soul,
Skimming across, feeling the whole.

Echoes of laughter, the sound of a sigh,
Ripples of joy that float and fly.
In this dance of feelings, we glide with grace,
Finding our rhythm, our sacred space.

Tethered to the Clouds

With threads of silver, we weave our dreams,
Tethered to clouds, where the sunlight beams.
Soft whispers carry our hopes so high,
Floating like feathers in the vast sky.

The world below fades, a distant muse,
As we drift through shades that warmly fuse.
In the embrace of the sky's gentle hand,
We find our hearts in a wonderland.

Reach for the Skies

With arms outstretched, we chase the light,
The dreams we hold take wondrous flight.
Above the clouds, our spirits soar,
In the vastness, we seek to explore.

Each star a whisper, secrets unfold,
Stories of courage, both brave and bold.
The horizon calls, a promise to keep,
In the depths of night, our hopes leap.

With every dawn, the sun will rise,
Painting the world in golden ties.
Together we'll climb, never be shy,
Hand in hand, we reach for the skies.

Our hearts aligned, we'll face the breeze,
In unity, we find our ease.
Bound by the dreams that lift us high,
Forever we'll strive, just you and I.

Reflections at Dusk

As twilight drapes in soft embrace,
The world transforms, a slowed-down pace.
Shadows dance, in colors warm,
Nature whispers, a soothing charm.

The river glimmers, a mirror's grace,
Echoes of light in a gentle trace.
Memories drift on the evening tide,
In the quiet dusk, our hearts abide.

Birds sing softly, their day now done,
Under the glow of a setting sun.
With every breath, the day takes flight,
In these reflections, everything feels right.

We pause to feel the fleeting hour,
In every moment, a blooming flower.
With dusk upon us, our souls ignite,
Together we wander, into the night.

A Dance through the Clouds

In a world where dreams collide,
We sway with the winds, with open pride.
Through the clouds, our laughter rings,
In the air, we find our wings.

The sun peeks in, a playful glance,
Every moment, a fleeting chance.
With each twirl, we paint the sky,
In this ballet, we learn to fly.

Whispers of joy in the softest breeze,
Moving together, just you and me.
Under the stars, we'll twinkle bright,
A dance through the clouds, igniting the night.

With every step, the world expands,
In harmony, we join our hands.
Floating free, as the moonlight glows,
In this euphoria, anything goes.

Scents of the Stratosphere

In the heights where dreams ignite,
Fragrant whispers dance in the night.
The essence of freedom fills the air,
In the stratosphere, we shed our care.

With every breath, the world reclaims,
The scents of adventure, wild and untamed.
From soaring peaks to valleys deep,
In each aroma, memories steep.

Petals and pine, a heady mix,
Nature's perfume, the heart it picks.
In this realm, where wishes sing,
Every scent brings a new beginning.

Embracing the winds, we'll chase the dawn,
With spirits bright, and hope reborn.
In the stratosphere, we feel alive,
With scents as our guide, together we thrive.

In the Arms of Altitude

Whispers of the high winds call,
Dreams take flight above it all.
Mountains cradle quiet sighs,
Echoes dance in open skies.

Horizon bends, the dusk begins,
Softest twilight, night's first sins.
Stars awake in subtle grace,
Guiding hearts to find their place.

Climbing higher, fears untie,
Breathless moments, spirits fly.
In the arms of boundless air,
Finding peace without a care.

Wrapped in warmth of nature's hand,
Dreamers walk on silent land.
Every step, a whispered prayer,
In the arms of altitude, share.

Boundless Softer Realities

Between the worlds, a doorway glows,
Where softer truths and wonder flows.
Each heartbeat whispers stories old,
Of visions wrapped in threads of gold.

Time drifts lightly, leaves no trace,
A gentle dance in sacred space.
Clouds pour dreams like gentle rain,
Filling hearts with joy and pain.

In quiet corners, shadows peek,
At boundless truths that softly speak.
Realities shift like sands at sea,
In every note, a melody.

Awakened minds embrace the light,
Finding magic in the night.
Boundless skies hold endless grace,
In softer worlds, our souls embrace.

Encounters in the Sky

Feathers drift on winds of fate,
Stars collide, and time waits late.
Where dreams mingle, hearts align,
In the vast sirens of design.

Clouds become a canvas wide,
Of whispered thoughts, we cannot hide.
Each encounter paints the air,
With stories anchored deep in care.

Glimmers of hope in twilight's glow,
Lightly woven where feelings flow.
In the sky, our spirits merge,
A symphony where souls converge.

With every pulse, a journey starts,
An orchestra of beating hearts.
Encounters etched in starlit skies,
Where love and destiny arise.

Navigating the Unknown

In misty shadows, paths entwine,
Questions linger, thoughts align.
With every step, the heart will race,
A dance with doubt, a steady pace.

Stars above, they guide the way,
The night whispers secrets to display.
Courage blooms, facing the void,
In the depths, dreams are deployed.

Turning tides, the storm will break,
Through the fears, I will awake.
Embrace the change, let shadows fade,
In the unknown, serenades are made.

Trust the journey, let it flow,
In silence, strength will grow.
Life unfolds, a vibrant hue,
Navigating paths both old and new.

A Celestial Journey

Wings unfurl beneath the stars,
On silver roads, past moons and Mars.
Galaxies spin, in cosmic dance,
A voyage sparked by a wishful glance.

Nebulae weave threads of light,
In the vastness, dreams take flight.
Constellations tell tales of old,
In whispered verses, the night is bold.

Stardust swirls, a gentle breeze,
Across the void, we glide with ease.
Each heartbeat marks the rhythm's flow,
In this embrace, our spirits glow.

Time suspends, as wonders bloom,
In the universe, there's no room for gloom.
A celestial path, forever bright,
Together we soar, in endless night.

Fading into Light

As shadows stretch across the floor,
Fading moments we can't ignore.
In twilight's hush, dreams softly sigh,
A gentle whisper, a fleeting high.

Colors blend in dusk's embrace,
A tapestry woven with time and space.
Memories linger, soft and warm,
In the stillness, we find our form.

To rise anew as dawn appears,
Letting go of hidden fears.
In the glow, hope takes its flight,
Transforming darkness, fading into light.

With every breath, the past reveals,
The strength of love, the heart that heals.
In radiant hues, our spirits ignite,
From shadows deep, we fade into light.

Gleaming Moments

In quiet corners, laughter hums,
Captured seconds, like beating drums.
A glance, a smile, the world ignites,
Gleaming moments, purest delights.

Sunrise breaks with golden grace,
A canvas painted, a warm embrace.
Time slips through our open hands,
In cherished pools where joy expands.

Fleeting whispers on the breeze,
Heartfelt stories in the trees.
Every heartbeat, a treasure trove,
In gleaming moments, love's song wove.

Like shimmering stars in the night sky,
We hold the fragments, letting them fly.
For life's mosaic, vibrant and bold,
Is built on moments, worth more than gold.

Transitions in the Twilight Sky

Pink hues blend with deepening blue,
Stars emerge, shy yet true.
Daylight wanes, a soft goodbye,
Embracing night, we breathe and sigh.

Clouds drift slowly, shadows cast,
Moments fleeting, fading fast.
Whispers dance on the evening air,
Introducing dreams, a subtle dare.

Moonlight spills like silver wine,
Guiding paths where thoughts align.
In the twilight's gentle hold,
Stories of the heart unfold.

As darkness deepens, souls awake,
Under the calm, the world will shake.
Transitions weave a tapestry,
In twilight's arms, we learn to be.

Breezes Carrying Secrets

Gentle zephyrs weave through trees,
Kissing leaves, they stir the ease.
Whispers linger in the air,
Stories told without a care.

Softly they carry hints of night,
Murmurs sweet, a hidden light.
In the rustle, a life unfolds,
Each breeze, a tale gently holds.

Through the grass, the secrets flow,
From the mountains high to valleys low.
Nature's breath, a soft caress,
In its touch, we find our rest.

Breezes come and breezes go,
Guardians of the tales we know.
In their dance, a world to see,
Carrying secrets, wild and free.

Colors of the Unseen

A spectrum hides behind the eyes,
In shadows deep, potential lies.
Vibrant shades of heart's desire,
Flicker softly, old and dire.

Through the mist, a blush of gold,
Quiet dreams begin to mold.
Yet unseen, the palette waits,
For bold strokes to reshape fates.

Each hue speaks a silent langue,
A melody sweet, a soothing song.
In the depths, rich stories brew,
Longing for a canvas new.

With every brushstroke, colors blend,
Echoes of a journey, no end.
In the unseen, beauty gleams,
Painting life with hopes and dreams.

Reflections in the Wind

Mirrored thoughts in rustling leaves,
Carried away, where the heart believes.
Upon the breeze, they swirl and play,
Whispering truths on a fleeting day.

Each gust stirs memories, old and wise,
Like shimmering light in a summer's rise.
Emotions dance in the autumn's chill,
In the wind's embrace, we find our will.

Through valleys filled with tender sighs,
The echoes of laughter softly rise.
Reflections blend in nature's song,
In this moment, we all belong.

As twilight deepens, shadows spin,
In the hush of night, we breathe within.
Reflections linger, calm and sweet,
In the wind, our souls meet.

Celestial Journeys in Emotion

Stars whisper tales of dreams,
In the silence of the night.
Every heartbeat shares its hopes,
Carried on the wings of light.

Moonlight dances on the sea,
Shimmering with memories past.
Time unwinds, a gentle breeze,
Emotions vast, forever cast.

Galaxies of laughter bloom,
In the heart's deep cosmic well.
Bridges born from joy and gloom,
Every story begins to swell.

Together we traverse the skies,
With wonder as our guiding spark.
In the cosmos, truth never lies,
Our souls shine bright against the dark.

Wings That Cradle Longing

A gentle flutter, soft and warm,
Promising a sweet embrace.
In the silence, hearts transform,
Finding solace in the space.

Wings spread wide upon the breeze,
Whispers of the dreams we chase.
In the stillness, longing frees,
Us to seek a brighter place.

Sorrow dances with the dawn,
Yet hope lingers, ever near.
In our hearts, the past is drawn,
Yet love's laughter starts to steer.

With every gust, our spirits lift,
Rising high above despair.
Together, we are love's own gift,
In the flight of the open air.

Velvet Skies of Reverie

Underneath a velvet cloak,
Stars weave tales of what could be.
Ethereal dreams gently spoke,
In the hush of twilight's spree.

Colors swirl in dusk's embrace,
Painting memories anew.
Every sigh, a soft touch space,
Where shadows and visions grew.

Echoes linger, breathless sights,
In the gaze of endless deep.
Wrapped within these velvet nights,
Dreams ignite while others sleep.

Waves of wonder roll and unfold,
Cradled by the moon's soft sway.
Within this realm, our hearts behold,
A tapestry of night and day.

Flapping Heartstrings

In the breeze, our wishes soar,
Carried by a tender song.
Each heartbeat whispers evermore,
In the rhythm where we belong.

Threads of love weave through the air,
Flapping gently, wild and free.
In every glance, a promise rare,
A melody meant just for me.

Life's sweet dance, a swirling flight,
With every flutter, hope ignites.
Together we embrace the night,
As heartstrings play, our souls unite.

In the canvas of the sky,
We paint dreams with every breath.
With wings that lift us high and nigh,
We find joy within love's depth.

Heartbeats Amidst the Clouds

In the soft light of dawn, we rise,
Gentle whispers drift in the skies.
Each heartbeat pulses, a sweet refrain,
Carried lightly on the subtle rain.

Dreams linger where the shadows play,
Hope dances in the break of day.
Every moment feels suspended there,
As we breathe in the sky's tender air.

Clouds embrace us, a warm cocoon,
Starlit songs fade with the moon.
Together we soar, hearts intertwined,
In this ephemeral world, unconfined.

With each heartbeat, we find our place,
Floating onward in this endless space.
Through the vast blue, we learn to glide,
In heartbeats, love's joy does abide.

Navigating the Invisible

Through the unseen paths we tread,
With every step, a silent thread.
Whispers of fate in the quiet air,
Guiding us softly, an unseen care.

Maps unfold in the back of our minds,
The heart understands what vision blinds.
Navigating waves of thought and fear,
Finding our way, the path becomes clear.

In the shadows where dreams converge,
The pulse of life begins to surge.
Trusting the pull of the intangible light,
Illuminating the dark with insight.

We journey forth, hand in hand,
Embracing the unknown, we stand.
In the invisible, we find our song,
Together we thrive, where we belong.

Aerial Portraits of Joy

High above the world we glide,
With laughter echoing, side by side.
Each moment captured, a frame of bliss,
In this tapestry of joy, we exist.

Colors swirl in the azure blue,
A canvas painted with me and you.
The sun kisses our smiles, so bright,
Days woven together in pure delight.

Birds sing tales from the windswept height,
Aerial melodies, soft and light.
Each heartbeat syncs with the sky's embrace,
In this portrait of joy, we find our place.

Floating freely on currents above,
In every glance, a whisper of love.
We are artists, crafting dreams on the fly,
In this world where our spirits can soar high.

The Flutter of Forgotten Wishes

In the corners of the heart, dreams sleep,
Wishes flutter, secrets to keep.
Memories linger like dew on grass,
Softly brushing by, moments that pass.

A sigh escapes as time stands still,
Whispers of hope on the wings of will.
Each wish a paper bird in flight,
Seeking the stars on a velvet night.

These forgotten dreams, we hold them dear,
Like shadows dancing, they draw us near.
With every beat, they stir the air,
Awakening stories of love and care.

Together we weave these dreams anew,
In the flutter of wishes, we pursue.
Hand in hand, through the twilight glow,
Finding the light in what we let go.

Veils of Gloom

Shadows whisper through the trees,
Quiet secrets on the breeze.
A shroud of mist, a silent plea,
In hidden corners, sorrows flee.

Faint echoes of a distant song,
Where the lost and lonely long.
Veils of black adorn the light,
Casting dreams in endless night.

Beneath the stars, a weeping heart,
Yearning for a brand-new start.
Yet in the dark, hope finds its way,
Guided by a flicker's sway.

Through the gloom, one must believe,
In twilight's grace, we shall weave.
A tapestry of joy and pain,
To dance beneath the pouring rain.

Dawn's Melancholy

The sun breaks through the morning haze,
With golden hues, it starts to blaze.
Yet shadows linger, soft and gray,
A bittersweet end to the day.

Waves of light caress the ground,
In quiet whispers, love is found.
But in that glow, a hint of tears,
For fleeting dreams and fading years.

The robin sings its waking call,
But echoes wear the silence's thrall.
As petals fall and colors fade,
The heart aches for the joy delayed.

In dawn's embrace, our sorrows blend,
A cycle that will never end.
Yet in this grief, we find the grace,
To cherish light and time's embrace.

Ascents of Euphoria

Upon the peaks where spirits soar,
We find the strength to seek for more.
With every step, we touch the sky,
In laughter's echo, we will fly.

The mountain's heart beats wild and free,
In euphoria's sweet decree.
With arms outstretched, we greet the sun,
Embracing joy, this race we've run.

Each breath, a gift of pure delight,
A canvas painted bold and bright.
Together we shall chase the dawn,
In wild abandon, we'll press on.

Through trails of gold, our spirits meld,
In celebration, hearts upheld.
Ascents of euphoria guide our way,
To brighter tomorrows, come what may.

Celestial Turmoil

Stars collide in cosmic rage,
Fate entwined on destiny's page.
Galaxies whirl in a dance so grand,
In chaos born, we take our stand.

Planets tremble in the void's breath,
In the silence, echoes of death.
Yet from the ashes, worlds are born,
In stardust dreams, new hopes are sworn.

The heavens twist, a grand facade,
In every mystery, our hearts applaud.
Through cosmic strife, we seek the light,
In turmoil's heart, we find our might.

In celestial storms, the soul ignites,
With every turn, our future writes.
Though chaos reigns, we stand as one,
In starlit paths, our journey's begun.

Canvas of Colors

Brushstrokes of red and gold,
A tapestry bright and bold.
Dreams painted wild in the sky,
Whispers of hues that will fly.

Every shade tells a tale,
Of love, of loss, and the frail.
Underneath the artist's hand,
Life's palette, bright and grand.

A canvas stretched, wide and free,
Where colors dance in jubilee.
Nature's chorus, soft and sweet,
In every stroke, the heart will beat.

As the day turns into night,
Stars emerge, a marvelous sight.
The canvas fades, but the dream,
Lives on in every vibrant gleam.

Swaying in the Atmosphere

Leaves rustle in a gentle breeze,
Whispers carried with such ease.
Dancing shadows, sunlight's kiss,
Nature's song, a sweet, soft bliss.

Clouds drift lazily in the sky,
Painting dreams as they fly high.
Colors merge, bright and light,
Swaying softly, day to night.

Every breath a soft embrace,
Moments linger, time slows pace.
In this world, we twirl and spin,
Finding joy in where we've been.

Together we sway, hand in hand,
Lost in wonder, across this land.
Every heartbeat a melody,
In the atmosphere, we are free.

Shadows of Dawn

Morning light, softly unfolds,
Casting shadows, secrets told.
Whispers of night, fading away,
As the sun greets a brand new day.

The horizon blushes, warm and bright,
Shadows dance with soft delight.
A canvas painted in soft gold,
Stories of tomorrow, yet to be told.

Birds take flight, a lively cheer,
With every note, they make it clear.
The dawn awakens, fresh and pure,
In its embrace, we shall endure.

Chasing shadows, seeking light,
Every moment feels so right.
In the morning's gentle glow,
We find the strength to grow.

Vibrations of Bliss

Softly, the echoes play a tune,
Twinkling like stars beneath the moon.
Harmonies of joy fill the air,
In this moment, without a care.

Rhythms pulse through every heart,
A symphony where dreams take part.
In the dance of life, we lose track,
Finding peace in the ebb and flow, no lack.

Colors swirl, feelings ignite,
In the vibrations, everything feels right.
Every laugh a note of grace,
In this harmony, we find our place.

Let the music guide our way,
With every beat, we'll gladly stay.
In the vibrations, pure and free,
We discover love's sweet harmony.

Serenades in the Wind

Whispers pass through lofty trees,
A melody that rides the breeze.
Soft sighs blend with twilight's glow,
As nature's song begins to flow.

Stars align in velvet skies,
While the moonlight gently lies.
Each note drifts on silken air,
Creating dreams beyond compare.

In the hush of the night, we stand,
Lost in love, hand in hand.
With every gust, hearts intertwine,
In the serenade, pure and divine.

Echoes of Tomorrow

Faint whispers of what is to be,
Call out softly, urging me.
In the shadows, futures gleam,
Fleeting glimpses of lost dreams.

Time flows like a river's bend,
Carrying hopes that never end.
Every heartbeat writes a tale,
In this world where memories sail.

Through the fog, I search and find,
The essence of a hopeful mind.
Each echo gives the strength to rise,
As dawn breaks with painted skies.

Crescendo of Fear

In the silence, whispers grow,
An unseen dread begins to show.
Shadows linger, dark and near,
Building something hard to bear.

Each heartbeat echoes loud and fast,
A haunting tune of shadows cast.
Through the night, a tension tight,
As courage dims and hope takes flight.

With every fear that grips the mind,
A battle fought, yet hard to find.
In the face of doubt, we stand,
As darkness looms, we take command.

Dancing on the Edge

We twirl upon the precipice bright,
Chasing dreams that dance in light.
Balancing on a fragile line,
Embracing both fear and divine.

With every step, we flirt with fate,
In this wild and wondrous state.
The void below, a sweet allure,
Calling us to be brave and sure.

Together we leap, hearts intertwined,
In this moment, unconfined.
For life is but a fleeting chance,
Let's celebrate this daring dance.

Elysian Breezes

In whispers soft, the breezes play,
They dance and twirl, a sweet ballet.
With every gust, a secret shared,
In Elysian fields, our hearts laid bare.

Through golden fields, the flowers sway,
Their colors bright, a rich display.
With scents of joy, they fill the air,
In nature's song, we lose our care.

The sunlight weaves through emerald trees,
A gentle warmth, a tender tease.
In playful winds, our laughter flows,
In Elysian dreams, our spirit grows.

So let us chase these breezes light,
In every moment, pure delight.
With hearts entwined, we drift and soar,
In Elysian fields, forevermore.

Chasing Daybreak

A dawn unfolds, with colors bright,
The world awakens, kissed by light.
With every step, we chase the sun,
A brand new day has now begun.

The sky ignites in shades of gold,
A story fresh, a tale retold.
We run through fields of morning dew,
Embracing dreams, both bold and true.

With every heartbeat, hopes arise,
In chasing daybreak, spirits fly.
We leave behind the darkened night,
As dawn bestows its gentle light.

Together we will seize the morn,
In every moment, love is born.
With hands entwined, we greet the day,
In chasing daybreak, come what may.

Trails of Tranquility

Through winding paths, the silence grows,
In nature's grip, the spirit flows.
With every step on soft earth laid,
On trails of peace, our worries fade.

The rustling leaves, a calming sound,
In tranquil woods, our hearts are found.
Beneath the sky, so vast and blue,
In every breath, we start anew.

With whispers of the gentle breeze,
We wander far, we seek the trees.
On trails where sunlight drips like gold,
Our souls connect, a tale unfolds.

In quiet moments, wisdom grows,
In nature's pause, true beauty shows.
With every step, our spirits sigh,
On trails of tranquility, we fly.

Lifting Spirits High

On wings of hope, we rise and soar,
With hearts ablaze, we seek for more.
In laughter's echo, joy will sing,
Together, we embrace the spring.

Through trials faced, we found our way,
In unity, we greet the day.
With every challenge, dreams ignite,
As spirits lift and take to flight.

With open hearts and arms spread wide,
In moments shared, we cast aside.
With every leap, we touch the sky,
In boundless joy, we're lifted high.

So let us dance beneath the stars,
A celebration of who we are.
With hands in hand, we'll face the tide,
In lifting spirits, love's our guide.

Skylines of Serenity

Above the city, quiet lights glow,
A canvas of calm, where dreams flow.
The stars whisper softly, their tales unfold,
In the night's embrace, a treasure to behold.

Gentle winds carry night's sweet song,
A lullaby where hearts belong.
Horizons stretch wide, hope takes flight,
With every breath, a chance to ignite.

Clouds drift slowly, painting the sky,
With hues of dusk as day waves goodbye.
A moment of peace, the soul's delight,
In the skylines of serenity, all feels right.

Reflections shimmer on waters deep,
Echoes of secrets that silence keeps.
Here in this realm, the spirit finds ease,
In the embrace of nature, life's gentle breeze.

Dance of the Tempest

Dark clouds gather, a warning cry,
Winds weave stories as they rise high.
Thunder rumbles, fierce and bold,
Nature's heartbeat, a tale retold.

Lightning flashes, a wild display,
Illuminating night, chasing shadows away.
The elements roar with untamed grace,
In the tempest's dance, there's fierce embrace.

Raindrops tumble, a rhythmic beat,
A symphony played on the pavement's sheet.
Chaos swirls, yet beauty remains,
In the storm's fury, life sustains.

When calm finally claims the night,
Stars peek through, a tranquil sight.
The tempest bows, its power withdrawn,
A dance once wild, now gently gone.

Feathered Reflections

In a quiet glade, shadows weave,
Amidst the trees, secrets believe.
A single feather drifts down slow,
Whispers of journeys, only it knows.

Birds take flight on horizons wide,
Painting the air, where songs abide.
Each graceful twist, a story spun,
In feathered reflections, dreams are won.

Fluttering softly on the breeze,
The dance of life brings hearts to ease.
Bright colors mesh, like thoughts on wing,
In the silent moments, nature will sing.

As twilight falls, a soft embrace,
Feathers glow in the dusky space.
Memory's echo, gentle and near,
In feathered reflections, all is clear.

Rhapsody in the Breeze

A melody weaves through branches high,
Swaying gently, the leaves reply.
Nature hums in a sweet refrain,
As day slips softly into the night's domain.

The sun sets low, painting the air,
Golden notes drift without a care.
Each whispering breeze tells a tale,
Of hopes and dreams that will not fail.

Stars blink alive in the velvet dark,
Marking the night with their bright spark.
A rhapsody plays, soft and free,
In the dance of shadows, lost in glee.

With every gust, the world seems kind,
Lifting spirits, untying the bind.
In each gentle sigh, love is released,
Creating a rhapsody, a moment of peace.

Currents of Emotion

Waves crash softly on the shore,
Feelings ebb and flow, forevermore.
Hearts wander lost in the tide,
Carried on the currents, we cannot hide.

Tears may fall like gentle rain,
Each drop echoes joy and pain.
In the depths, true colors show,
As we navigate the ebb and flow.

Moments fleeting, like a breeze,
In tangled thoughts we find our ease.
Through the storms, we learn to sail,
Driven by love, we will not fail.

On this journey of the heart,
Every ending sparks a new start.
Emotions dance like shadows cast,
A beautiful reminder of the past.

Soaring Through Shadows

Beneath the weight of looming night,
Hope ignites with a distant light.
With every breath, we learn to rise,
Soaring high through darkened skies.

Whispers linger on the breeze,
Guiding us towards our dreams with ease.
In the silence, courage blooms,
Filling hearts, dispelling glooms.

Across the chasm, we'll take flight,
Chasing stars that pierce the night.
Fear melts away with each new dawn,
In shadows' dance, we will be drawn.

Together we shall face the storm,
In every cold embrace, there's warmth.
Soaring high, we'll break the chains,
Finding peace where hope remains.

Driftwood Dreams

Once a tree, stood tall and proud,
Now it drifts, tucked in a shroud.
Carried forth by currents strong,
Whispers of where it once belonged.

With each turn, it tells a tale,
Of endless journeys through the gale.
Held by tides, beloved by time,
Each splinter shares a rhythm and rhyme.

Anchored not, to any shore,
Seeking places to explore.
A vessel of memories half-remembered,
In dreams of driftwood, hope's embers glittered.

In the quiet, hearts may find,
The sacred bond of the unconfined.
So let us drift on waves of fate,
Embracing love that will not wait.

Celestial Whirlwinds

In the night, where stardust swirls,
Galaxies spin, like hidden pearls.
A cosmic dance of fate and chance,
We twirl within this vast expanse.

Planets sing in harmony,
Notes of light, a symphony.
In the silence of the night,
Dreams take flight, a wondrous sight.

Through swirling mists of time and space,
We chase the stars, a thrilling race.
In the whirlwinds, truths unfold,
Stories of destinies yet untold.

As we soar on winds divine,
Each heart a star, forever shine.
In celestial realms, we're free,
Boundless as the endless sea.

Celestial Rustle of Sentiments

In the quiet night, stars awaken,
Whispers of dreams softly taken.
Echoes of hearts begin to dance,
In the moonlight's gentle trance.

Leaves of silver sway and gleam,
Moonlit paths where lovers dream.
A soft breeze carries tales of old,
Love's sweet secrets, gently told.

In the stillness, sighs emerge,
Gentle currents, a tender surge.
Hearts entwined in whispered verse,
A universe, a love diverse.

Amongst the stardust, shadows play,
Each moment cherished, night and day.
Celestial rustle, sweet refrain,
Threads of emotion, held in grain.

The Ascent of Hope's Horizon

Through valleys deep and mountains high,
We chase the light, we learn to fly.
With burdened hearts, we take our stand,
Together, we rise, hand in hand.

The dawn breaks gently, skies ablaze,
A tapestry of hope displays.
In every shade, a saga spun,
The ascent begins as night is done.

Fingers stretched towards the sun,
In every battle, we have won.
With every climb, we shed our doubt,
The voice of hope begins to shout.

As horizon glows with promise bright,
The world awakens to new light.
With hearts ignited, we find our way,
Marching forward, come what may.

Whispers of the Sky

Clouds drift by in serene repose,
Carrying tales that time bestows.
Each breeze a note, each star a word,
In the silence, secrets are heard.

Twilight dances on velvet air,
Echoes of thoughts drifting with care.
Underneath the vast expanse, we dwell,
Finding comfort in stories we tell.

Above the chaos, peace resides,
In whispers of dreams where hope abides.
A canvas painted with hues of light,
Guides our souls through the deep night.

Stars like lanterns, guide our flight,
With every whisper, we ignite.
The sky reveals our hidden dreams,
In celestial whispers, life redeems.

Wings of Solitude

In the stillness, a heart takes flight,
Carried on wings of solitude's light.
Beneath the sky so vast and wide,
In quiet moments, we confide.

Like a feather on a gentle breeze,
Drifting softly with grace and ease.
Finding solace in the space around,
In silence, our true selves are found.

A hidden strength within the calm,
In solitude's arms, a healing balm.
Through whispered thoughts, we learn to soar,
Embracing the silence, longing for more.

Wings of solitude, strong and free,
In the still air, we simply be.
Each solitary journey, a sacred thread,
We rise above, where dreams are spread.

Currents of Reflection

In the stillness of the night,
Whispers ride the silver streams,
Thoughts drift like leaves in flight,
Carried by the weight of dreams.

Mirrors of the starlit sky,
Show the tales of days gone by,
Each ripple holds a secret deep,
In waters where the shadows sleep.

Time weaves stories in the flow,
Where old memories softly glow,
Glimmers pulse with every wave,
Echoes of the hearts that brave.

As the dawn begins to break,
New reflections start to wake,
In the light, their truths revealed,\nCurrents wise, and hearts healed.

Aerial Secrets

High above in azure hue,
Clouds are draped like dreams untold,
Whispered secrets drift anew,
Carried softly, warm and bold.

Feathers dance in gentle breeze,
Wings of hope that soar and glide,
Messages the sky foresees,
In the currents where they bide.

Echoes of a silent prayer,
Stretched between the earth and sky,
Lessons learned in layers rare,
Where the heart can learn to fly.

The horizon holds a spell,
In the vastness, stories swell,
Aerial tales of love and grace,
In every breath, the sky's embrace.

The Pulse of the Sky

Heartbeat echoes in the blue,
A rhythmic dance of light and air,
Nature sings of life anew,
In the pulse, the world laid bare.

Stars align, a cosmic beat,
Each twinkle sings a song of light,
Beneath the heavens, time is sweet,
In the dark, the heart takes flight.

Shadows play and whisper low,
Guided by the moon's soft gaze,
Every moment, ebb and flow,
In the sky's eternal maze.

Feel the thrum of day and night,
As the universe unfolds wide,
In the glow of dawn's first light,
The pulse of dreams will be our guide.

Windswept Memories

Among the hills where breezes sigh,
Echoes of laughter drift and roam,
Whispers of days that flutter by,
Carried on the winds back home.

Golden fields where shadows dance,
Time unwinds in gentle waves,
Remnants of a fleeting chance,
In every gust, a memory saves.

On the path that winds away,
Footprints left in soft, sweet grass,
Sunlit moments, bright as day,
In the winds they softly pass.

So let the breezes softly weave,
Tales of love and joy we crave,
In windswept memories, believe,
Time's embrace, a heart to save.

The Airborne Palette of Dreams

Colors dance in the twilight sky,
Brushes dipped in hope and sighs.
Winds carry whispers of the night,
Painting visions, taking flight.

Golden hues begin to blend,
Crafting tales that never end.
Each stroke tells a secret tale,
In the breeze, dreams set sail.

Clouds morph into shapes unseen,
Sketching wishes where we've been.
A canvas vast, our hearts provide,
In this world, our spirits ride.

From dawn's light to dusk's embrace,
These colored realms, a timeless space.
With every breath, our dreams unfold,
An airborne palette, bright and bold.

When Clouds Confess

In the hush of a gentle breeze,
Clouds gather, stirring thoughts with ease.
Whispers tumble from high above,
Secrets shared with those they love.

Silver linings, truth revealed,
Darkened shadows, fears concealed.
Raindrops fall like tears of grace,
Soft confessions in their place.

As storms gather, hearts are bare,
Nature's breath, a sacred prayer.
Thunder speaks of emotions near,
While lightning sparks the hopes we steer.

When the skies spill their soul's delight,
We too learn to confess our plight.
In every cloud, a tale awaits,
As they share, the heart resonates.

Starlit Whispers of the Heart

Stars twinkle in the midnight air,
Whispers gentle, a cosmic prayer.
Each glimmer holds a secret wish,
In the vastness, dreams we cherish.

Beneath the moon's soft celestial glow,
Our hearts converse, soft and slow.
In silence shared, connections grow,
Bound by magic we both know.

Galaxies spin with tales unspoken,
Each twinkling light, a heart's token.
Woven into the night so fine,
Starlit whispers, yours and mine.

As dawn approaches, shadows fade,
Yet the echoes of love are made.
In the universe's tender art,
We find our truths, a work of heart.

The Symphony of Sunlit Emotions

Golden rays begin to play,
Crafting melodies of the day.
Nature hums a joyful tune,
Beneath the warmth of the bright moon.

Birds sing sweet in fleeting flight,
Voices echo, pure delight.
With every note, our spirits rise,
Igniting hope beneath the skies.

Flowers bloom in vibrant hues,
Dancing softly to the muse.
Raindrops laugh and sunbeams sway,
Creating symphonies in a grand array.

In this concert of life's embrace,
Each feeling finds its rightful place.
As sunlight breaks through the dawn,
We celebrate till hope is drawn.

Gossamer Waves

Soft whispers kiss the shore,
With secrets held in foam.
Dancing light on water's face,
Reflects the sky's wide dome.

Glistening trails of silver spark,
As the wind begins to play.
Nature's brush with gentle strokes,
Sings of night and day.

Gentle ripples call my name,
In the twilight's tender glow.
Each wave a fleeting moment,
A memory to bestow.

In this realm where dreams collide,
I wander, lost and free.
Gossamer waves beckon me,
To join their reverie.

Tides of Yearning

In shadows deep where dreams reside,
I hear the ocean's sigh.
Each wave a heartbeat's echo,
A whisper passing by.

The pull of love, a distant call,
Draws me to the sea.
With every rise and fall of tide,
I long for what could be.

Footprints fade upon the sand,
Yet memories remain.
Waves of longing stretch to meet,
My heart's relentless pain.

Moonlit nights, they paint my soul,
With shades of hope and grief.
Tides of yearning wash ashore,
In every falling leaf.

Ethereal Journeys

Across the fabric of the night,
I sail on starlit streams.
In realms where time and space collide,
I dance among my dreams.

Whispers stir in cosmic winds,
Carrying tales untold.
Every twinkle, every glow,
A story to unfold.

In this vast and boundless sky,
I drift on silver beams.
Ethereal journeys stretch afar,
Beyond what daylight seems.

With each heartbeat, I ascend,
To worlds both strange and bright.
In the hush of endless night,
I find my soul's true light.

Flights of Fancy

On wings of thought, I rise and soar,
Through skies of endless blue.
Every cloud a soft retreat,
In visions soft and true.

Whirling dreams like autumn leaves,
Dance upon the breeze.
With joy I chase the fleeting light,
And wander where I please.

Imagination sets me free,
From bounds of daily life.
With every flight, a new delight,
Beyond all worldly strife.

In vibrant hues of hope I glide,
Through realms of pure romance.
Flights of fancy lead me on,
To where my spirit prance.

Wings of Whispered Emotion

In twilight's glow, emotions rise,
Gentle whispers fill the skies.
Hearts unfold, like petals fair,
Carried softly on the air.

The breeze will tell of dreams untold,
Secrets in the night so bold.
With every sigh, the world ignites,
As hope takes flight on wings of light.

Through shadows deep, they drift and sway,
Eclipsing doubts that fade away.
A dance of thoughts, pure and true,
In every flutter, I find you.

The moon observes with tender gaze,
As we embrace this fleeting phase.
Wings of whisper, soft and free,
In silence, we find our harmony.

Soaring Shadows of the Heart

In the stillness, shadows play,
Echoes of what words can't say.
The heart beats strong, yet soft as mist,
In every glance, a fleeting twist.

As memories dance like faint reflections,
Soaring high through deep connections.
Every sigh a bridge to cross,
Among the tides of love and loss.

With gentle grace, they take their flight,
Whispers linger in the night.
Our souls entwined, a sacred art,
Soaring shadows of the heart.

Through a labyrinth of dreams we roam,
In every heartbeat, we find home.
United still, though miles apart,
With every beat, we share our heart.

Transient Tides of Feeling

Upon the shore, where waves embrace,
Transient tides, a flowing grace.
Moments rise like tides so bold,
While stories of the heart unfold.

The sun dips low, a fleeting sight,
Casting gold upon the night.
In every breath, emotions swell,
Each tide a new tale to tell.

Through storms that crash and calm that stays,
Feelings shift in myriad ways.
Yet in the depths, we find the spark,
Illuminating paths through dark.

As we drift with currents wild,
Life's waves remind us, love's a child.
Transient tides, both calm and keen,
In waves of feeling, we are seen.

A Dance in the Ether

In ethereal realms, we find our way,
A dance of light at the break of day.
With every move, the cosmos sways,
In harmony, we chase the rays.

The stars align in cosmic flow,
Guiding whispers soft and slow.
With every step, the world transforms,
In this dance, our spirit warms.

Through galaxies of dreams we spin,
In every twist, a new begin.
The universe, our endless stage,
A dance in the ether, free from cage.

As dawn breaks forth with colors bright,
We celebrate this sacred night.
In every pulse, a story told,
A dance in the ether, brave and bold.

Chasing the Drift of Dusk

As day gives way to soft embrace,
The sun retreats, a gentle chase.
Shadows stretch and colors blend,
Night whispers sweet, the daylight's end.

Through twilight's glow, the dreams do stir,
A fragrant breeze, a touch of blur.
Stars twinkle shy, in velvet skies,
A canvas painted with silent sighs.

The horizon swallows fiery light,
Fleeting moments take to flight.
In this hush, the heart can thrum,
Chasing echoes where thoughts succumb.

With every step, a story told,
In fading light, the brave and bold.
We wander forth, through dusk's embrace,
In search of peace, we find our place.

The Hues of Fleeting Thoughts

A palette rich with dreams untold,
Brushstrokes of light in hues of gold.
Whispers dance on canvas bare,
A symphony of thoughts laid where.

Moments flutter like butterflies,
Each one glints with fierce goodbyes.
In shades of blue and scarlet red,
The mind's own art, a path we tread.

Time drips slow in morning's dew,
Colors shift, and yet remain true.
In fleeting dreams, we catch a glimpse,
Of vibrant worlds where passion wimps.

So paint your heart with wild delight,
In strokes of day, and depths of night.
For every thought, a vivid hue,
In fleeting moments, life feels new.

Suspended in Elysian Breezes

Drifting gently on the air,
A melody that holds me there.
Elysian whispers, soft and sweet,
In every breath, our hearts do meet.

The world around fades to a hum,
In this embrace, peace has come.
Through branches swaying, leaves take flight,
Suspended moments, pure delight.

With every sigh, the spirit soars,
Beyond the shores, to distant wars.
In breezes soft, the soul finds grace,
A quiet haven, a sacred space.

Let time dissolve in gentle glow,
In breezes where the wildflowers grow.
Suspended high, our dreams released,
In Elysium, we find our feast.

Skylines of the Soul

Beneath the arch of endless skies,
We trace the lines where the spirit flies.
In silhouettes of dreams we chase,
The skyline stretches, full of grace.

Each star a map of hopes once shared,
In twilight's quilt, our hearts laid bare.
With every pulse, the night reveals,
The hidden truths that time conceals.

As shadows dance to the moon's soft glow,
In quietude, our thoughts ebb and flow.
Skylines stretch, horizons wide,
A journey taken side by side.

Together we weave a tapestry,
Of moments stitched in unity.
In every dawn, our souls unite,
Chasing the skyline into the light.

Moonlit Reverie

Beneath the sky of silver hue,
The whispers of the night renew.
Stars dance upon the velvet sea,
In dreams, I wander, wild and free.

The cool breeze carries tales untold,
Of mysteries in shadows bold.
Guiding hearts to realms divine,
Where love and hope forever shine.

A tapestry of light unfolds,
In secret nights, the magic holds.
Each glow a promise, soft and clear,
In moonlit dreams, I find you near.

So let the silver beams embrace,
With every flicker, find your place.
In the reverie, we both shall dwell,
In whispered thoughts, all is well.

Flutters of Hope

Amidst the fields where wildflowers grow,
Tiny creatures dance to nature's flow.
With every flutter, dreams take flight,
In sunlit mornings, hearts feel light.

The world awakens to gentle grace,
In every petal, a warm embrace.
A symphony of colors bright,
Paints the canvas of pure delight.

Hope springs eternal like the dawn,
In the soft glow, fears are drawn.
Like butterflies that greet the day,
Each moment holds a chance to play.

So let the flutters guide our way,
In every heart, a brighter ray.
With love as light, our spirits soar,
In unison, forevermore.

Airborne Whispers

On gusts of wind, secrets sway,
Carried softly, they drift away.
They weave through trees, a gentle song,
In their embrace, we all belong.

Soft rustlings in the quiet night,
Stirring dreams with pure delight.
The whispers dance on zephyr's breath,
Defying silence, conquering death.

In every sigh, there lies a tale,
Of laughter shared, of journeys pale.
A call to souls, to fly, to roam,
In the whispers, we find our home.

So listen close, let spirits rise,
In airborne whispers, seek the skies.
For every breath holds endless chance,
In nature's song, we find our dance.

Stirring the Twilight

As day dips low and shadows blend,
A tapestry of hues, we mend.
The twilight breathes a calming sigh,
As dusk unfurls the evening sky.

With colors swirling, time stands still,
The heart awakens, dreams fulfill.
In soft transitions, hope takes flight,
Guiding us through the gentle night.

Stars begin to pierce the gloom,
Each spark a promise, life to bloom.
In twilight's grasp, we find our peace,
As day and night in love increase.

So let the whispers of night enfold,
In twilight's arms, our stories told.
With every heartbeat, let it flow,
In the magic of the twilight glow.

The Canvas of Euphoria

In colors bright, the dreams unfold,
Each stroke a story, joy retold.
With laughter dipped in golden light,
The canvas dances, pure and bright.

Each hue a whisper, soft and sweet,
A palette rich where moments meet.
In every shade, the heart takes flight,
In vibrant strokes, we find our light.

Beyond the frame, the spirits soar,
A world of wonder to explore.
With every brush, a feeling pours,
The canvas speaks, forevermore.

In this embrace of vivid grace,
We lose ourselves in time and space.
The canvas sings, a joyous sound,
In euphoria, we're truly found.

Fluctuations in a Celestial Tide

Waves of stars in cosmic dance,
Galaxies spin, a timeless prance.
The moonlight glistens on the sea,
In ebb and flow, we find the key.

As comets streak through velvet skies,
They carry secrets, whispers, sighs.
In stellar currents, hearts are tied,
To the rhythm of the celestial tide.

Planets wander, dreams take flight,
In cosmic realms beyond our sight.
Each rise and fall, a tale unspun,
In this vastness, we are one.

Eons pass in silent grace,
Yet time holds fast, a warm embrace.
In fluctuations, we reside,
In the harmony of the celestial tide.

Currents of the Mind

Thoughts like rivers, flowing free,
Meander gently, wild and free.
In currents deep, ideas clash,
A torrent swift, a fleeting flash.

Reflections dance upon the stream,
In every ripple, a silent dream.
With every twist, a new design,
The currents weave the heart and mind.

In eddies form, the chaos brews,
Yet in the whirl, a clarity ensues.
Through winding paths, we seek to find,
The treasure hid in the currents of the mind.

With every surge, a lesson learned,
In currents' ebb, the fire burned.
To navigate this vast expanse,
Is to embrace the mind's great dance.

Ephemeral Echoes Above

Whispers linger in the air,
Soft and fleeting, light as care.
In moments brief, they come alive,
Like shadows cast where dreams derive.

Echoes fade, yet still they sing,
In lengthy silence, memories cling.
They dance like leaves upon the breeze,
In whispers soft, they aim to please.

In twilight hours, they weave through night,
A tapestry of subtle light.
With each heartbeat, they intertwine,
Ephemeral, yet they define.

These echoes paint the world in gold,
Stories of the brave and bold.
Though transient, they leave their mark,
In echoes bright, we find the spark.

Whirlwinds of Nostalgia

Memories swirl like leaves in fall,
Whispers of laughter beckon my soul.
Time's tender touch feels like a call,
In moments lost, I find myself whole.

Footprints traced in the sands of yore,
Each echo a pulse of days gone by.
I wander through doors forevermore,
Chasing shadows beneath the sky.

The soft embrace of a fleeting glance,
Cradles my heart in a wistful dance.
Caught in a dream, lost in romance,
The past's gentle grip holds me in trance.

Whirlwinds of memories, fierce yet sweet,
Guide me through pathways only I roam.
Where every heartbeat finds its repeat,
In the warmth of the places I call home.

Silhouettes Against the Sky

Against the dusk, the figures stand still,
Tall and bold, where shadows align.
Whispers of night beckon a thrill,
Silhouettes dance, with secrets entwined.

Stars awaken, painting the night,
Each twinkle a story, a dream untold.
In the soft glow, they find their light,
Tracing the past, their stories unfold.

Beneath the moon, their silence sings,
Echoes of laughter in twilight's embrace.
Time stands still on a web of strings,
In the stillness, I find my place.

Dreamers and lovers, lost in the glow,
Silhouettes weave tales of longing and grace.
In the vastness, their shadows will flow,
Forever etched in the night's gentle face.

The Weight of Clouds

Softly they gather, a blanket above,
Veiling the sun with a whispering sigh.
Each droplet holds a promise of love,
The weight of clouds, where wishes lie.

They drift in silence, cradling the sky,
Drawing the world into shadows deep.
In their embrace, the soft moments fly,
As I surrender to thoughts I keep.

Colors blend in a canvas of grey,
A painting of dreams, both heavy and light.
A lullaby sung at the end of the day,
Inviting the stars to break through the night.

The weight of clouds, a burden of grace,
Holds the echoes of rain yet to come.
In their soft folds, I find my safe space,
As the symphony plays, inviting the hum.

Glimmers in the Gloom

In the heart of darkness, a flicker appears,
Glimmers that dance in the shadows so deep.
They weave through the silence, quieting fears,
A promise of light that the night shall keep.

Each twinkle whispers of stories untold,
Of hope and despair intertwined in the night.
In the folds of dusk, the brave and the bold,
Carry their dreams on the wings of twilight.

Through the mist, they shimmer, a timeless embrace,
Every spark holds the weight of a prayer.
In the gloom, I seek solace and space,
For glimmers remind me that light can be rare.

So I gather my courage, pursue what I must,
In the dark, every shimmer ignites a new path.
Glimmers in the gloom, a return to the trust,
That light will emerge from the echoes of wrath.

Echoes of the Heart

In the chambers where secrets lie,
Whispers of dreams softly sigh.
Memories linger, faint yet bold,
Stories of love in silence told.

Time flows like a gentle stream,
Carrying fragments of a dream.
Hearts entwined in the dance of fate,
Echoes resound as we contemplate.

Lost in shadows that softly cast,
The warmth of a touch from the past.
Each heartbeat, a song of old,
In the silence, the tales unfold.

Within the stillness, hope ignites,
Guiding us through the endless nights.
Echoes linger, never apart,
Forever bound, the echoes of the heart.

Clouds of Unease

Darkened skies with a heavy breath,
Whispers of doubt dance with a threat.
Shadows linger, lost in the gray,
Clouds of unease won't drift away.

Fleeting moments of joy now fade,
Echoes of laughter in twilight shaded.
Raindrops gather, heavy with fears,
Painting the world with unshed tears.

Lightning strikes in a tempest's rage,
Turning the calm to a frenzied stage.
Hope clings tight like the sun in the west,
Yearning for peace, for a moment of rest.

Yet amidst the storm, the light will break,
Washing away, all the hearts that ache.
Clouds will part as the dawn does rise,
Revealing the beauty hidden in lies.

Beneath the Feathered Veil

Secrets hidden in shadows deep,
Beneath a veil where silence sleeps.
Feathers soft as the twilight breeze,
Whispers of comfort that aim to please.

In twilight's arms, where dreams take flight,
Beneath the stars that grace the night.
A world unfolds in muted hues,
Nature sings of ancient truths.

With every rustle, a tale to share,
Of love and loss, of hope and care.
Fleeting moments, soft and pale,
Embrace the night beneath the veil.

In the twilight, let hearts reveal,
The strength that lies beneath the feel.
Together we soar, unafraid, unbroken,
Beneath the feathered veil, unspoken.

Horizon of Longings

As dawn awakens the silent sea,
A horizon stretches, wild and free.
Longings whisper on the gentle tide,
Dreams unfold where hopes reside.

Each wave a heartbeat, a rhythmic call,
Echoing wishes that rise and fall.
With every breath, a future bright,
Painting the sky in colors of light.

Footprints linger on the sandy shore,
Stories of journeys, longing for more.
Under the sun, our spirits soar,
Chasing the sun to the distant shore.

In the distance, where dreams unite,
A horizon gleams with pure delight.
Together we chase, love as our guide,
On this endless path, side by side.